Nonprofit Crowdfunding Explained

By Salvador Briggman

Copyright © 2016 Salvador Briggman LLC

All rights reserved. No part of this publication may be reproduced, distributed, or transmitted in any form or by any means, including photocopying, recording, or other electronic or mechanical methods, without the prior written permission of the publisher, except in the case of brief quotations embodied in critical reviews and certain other noncommercial uses permitted by copyright law

Although the author and publisher have made every effort to ensure that the information in this book was correct at press time, the author and publisher do not assume and hereby disclaim any liability to any party for any loss, damage, or disruption caused by errors or omissions, whether such errors or omissions result from negligence, accident, or any other cause.

The book is not intended for use as a source of legal or financial advice. You should always consult legal and financial professionals to provide specific guidance in evaluating and pursing investment or business opportunities. The advice, examples, and strategies in this book are not suitable for every situation. The materials are not intended to represent or guarantee desired results.

http://www.crowdcrux.com

Introduction

Right now, we're in the middle of a **_historic shift_** in charitable giving behavior. The rules of nonprofit fundraising are being rewritten as we speak. With the emergence of social media, smartphones, and the web, opportunities for budding nonprofits are finally opening up. What were once tried and true methods to engage donors are quickly becoming archaic and ineffective.

Believe it or not, you are living in the golden age of fundraising. A handful of nonprofits have caught on and are absolutely crushing it online. They've harnessed the power of technology to run massive online giving campaigns and reach thousands of supporters across the web. It's a complete no-brainer, but not everyone realizes that yet.

In the next few pages I'm going to be introducing you to several of these organizations that have caught on to and are riding a soaring trend. I've written about many of these orgs on my popular blog, which has been cited by the New York Times, the Wall Street Journal, and more. I've also spoken with many on my podcast.

After talking with these nonprofits, I realized one thing. They're not special. What they're doing isn't all that sophisticated. They're run by ordinary folks, just like you and me. In fact, if you follow the steps that I outline in this book, you'll be able to replicate their results. You'll finally get badly needed funding for your organization.

Take a second to imagine just how great it will feel to log on to your computer and find your email inbox overflowing with donation messages. Wouldn't that be awesome?

Instead, maybe you'll be at a restaurant, having dinner with a prospective donor. Suddenly, you'll feel your phone start to buzz. As you take it out, you'll see your screen flooded with app notifications. Confused, you'll start to read them one by one.

"... just donated to your campaign! Congratulations!"

People are actually giving money online to **your** fundraising campaign. It isn't pocket change either. These are significant sums.

At that moment, you'll finally realize the power of crowdfunding. You don't have to physically be there to attract new donors. Wow!

I'm not saying that it's going to be easy. Quite frankly, you're going to be treading into uncharted waters. A lot of the tools, websites, and techniques I'm about to cover might seem unfamiliar and at first, confusing. But, I promise you that I'll hold your hand every step of the way.

By the end of this ebook, you'll have a clear step-by-step plan for executing an online crowdfunding campaign and know what to do next. More importantly, you'll be able to stay true your org's mission and serve humanity.

- Sal

P.S. Here's the bonus video if you want to watch that first. (https://www.youtube.com/watch?v=9wIZkJ5a62E)

Table of Contents

Chapter 1: Online Giving Revolution 1
Chapter 2: Crowdfunding Success Stories 8
Chapter 3: Choosing a Platform 16
Chapter 4: Making a Great Campaign 25
Chapter 5: Mastering Donor Psychology 36
Chapter 6: Marketing Your Campaign 46
Chapter 7: Starting a New Nonprofit 65
Chapter 8: Conclusion 73

Chapter 1: Online Giving Revolution

In 2014, Blackbaud surveyed 3,000+ nonprofit organizations and released a study on charitable giving. The report showed that overall, charitable giving revenue grew by 4.9% in 2013. Sounds respectable, right?

However, compared to 2012, **online giving** grew by 13.5%, with the largest amount of growth happening in small nonprofits to the tune of 18.4%. This is the second year that online giving has shown a double-digit growth rate. Although online giving only accounted for 6.4% of all charitable giving in 2013, it is the fastest growing sector, particularly among faith-based organizations and smaller nonprofits.

What does this mean? Even though tried and true methods of fundraising work and brought in over $10 billion dollars for nonprofits in this study, the power of the internet, smartphones, and an increasingly social media savvy donor base is changing the fundraising game, and you need to take notice.

The Rate of Smartphone Adoption

You'd be hard-pressed to find an inventor in 1900 that would have predicted that even a child could hold all of the world's cumulative knowledge in the palm of their hand by the first decade of the 21st Century. But, that's exactly what a smartphone is: a miniature computer that lets you stay connected 24/7, whether you're at home or on the go.

More and more, millennials and young working professionals are no longer turning to their computer, the radio, or even the TV for entertainment. They're checking their Facebook feed from their phone, going on SnapChat, browsing Instagram, or reading up on the latest news on Twitter. A person's attention, the most sought after commodity, is more difficult to maintain than ever before.

According to Nielsen's 2013 study, the smartphone penetration rate has reached 64 percent in the United States, with 80 percent of new buyers choosing a smartphone as their mobile handset device. This estimate is backed up by the PewResearchCenter, which pegged smartphone adoption at 56% of the American adult population in 2013. However, since then, there have been claims that the US has reached a "smartphone saturation" point and is now seeing a rate of 75% smartphone penetration.

In fact, smartphone adoption is on the rise all over the world. eMarketer recently released a study citing that the number of smartphones worldwide will surpass 2 billion in 2016, which is in line with BusinessInsider's report that nearly 22% of the world population owned a smartphone in 2013.

Yes, this means that your son or daughter now can play games all the time, have two-way video calls with their friends, and easily capture the moments that matter to them, with interesting photo filters or captions. But, it also that the way in which we receive, spread, and process news has fundamentally shifted as a society.

The Rise of The Social Web

Arguably, the worldwide web has had three major phases. The first being an information consumption phase. During this time, you could check out your friend's nonprofit website, which was mainly static, get information and click around a few links. It functioned as a glorified brochure that was a small complimentary feature to getting a real brochure in the mail, watching video tapes, seeing TV ads, or calling up the actual office.

Next, we began to see the rise of search engines, bloggers, and online transactions. Search engines, particularly Google, made it easy to connect with organizations that you cared about or to learn more about particular causes. You might forward an email to your friend, receive an email chain letter, or comment on a particular news story. In addition, you might have read or run a personal online blog, which has other readers and has opinions on ongoing events. In fact, as of 2014, 6.7 million people actively blog and 77% of internet users read blogs.

Although online transactions have always been met with a bit of skepticism, everyday internet users were beginning to become accustomed to the idea of purchasing items online, which may have been recommended by a blogger, or that they found while searching on Google.

We've entered the day of the social web, where smartphones, online video, high quality websites, and social networks like Facebook, Twitter, and YouTube are changing up the fundraising game. Now, an individual doesn't need a blog, website, or even YouTube channel to share the stories and causes that they care about. They can do it with the click of a button from their Facebook account.

According to Digital Insights, as of 2014, Facebook has over 1 billion monthly active mobile users, which is comprised of 75% of adults. In addition, over 500 million tweets are sent per day with 78% active on mobile devices. Although a newer social network, Instagram already has over 200 million monthly active users and 20+ Billion photos have been shared on Instagram to date. Finally, the video viewing and sharing network YouTube, which was founded in 2005, has already amassed over 1 billion users, with 40% of YouTube traffic coming from mobile.

As one of the newer social networks, Instagram has only been around since 2010, but represents the beginning of a new trend towards the socialization of the mobile device. In fact, SnapChat, which was founded in 2011, has reported that users send 700 million photos per day and that Snapchat Stores are viewed 500 million times per day, now with the addition of notable networks like CNN, the Food Network, National Geographic, Yahoo News, and more.

A tidal wave is beginning to form that will change online giving and donor relations as we know it. The question is not if it's going to happen. The question is how will you respond. Will you surf on the top of the new wave or be drawn beneath its depths?

The Success of The ALS Ice Bucket Challenge

In 2014, the world witnessed the success of "The ALS Ice Bucket Challenge," which ended up raising $100 million dollars for the ALS Association, which helps bring awareness to and advocate for patients that have suffered from issues related to amyotrophic lateral sclerosis (ALS), also known as Lou Gehrig's disease.

The challenge, which turned overnight into a worldwide sensation, was simple. As a Facebook user, you might be nominated by a friend or acquaintance to participate in the ALS Ice Bucket Challenge. Within 24 hours of being nominated, you could either donate $100 to help combat ALS or video tape yourself pouring a bucket of ice water on your head. In many cases, high net worth individuals chose to do both. After participating in the challenge, you would have the chance to nominate up to three other participants who would then need to complete the challenge within 24 hours.

These simple rules and the time-sensitive nature of the challenge turned a small effort to help raise awareness for ALS into a growing snowball. By the end of social media tsunami, there were 2.4 million tagged videos circulating Facebook. Celebrities including Bill Gates, Barak Omaba, George W. Bush, Matt Damon, LeBron James, and more had participated in the movement.

Although there have been criticisms that the challenge focused more on "having fun" than cultivating the habit of lifelong charitable contribution, it's clear that social media and the internet has completely transformed nonprofit giving behaviors. While once brochures, physical mail, and personal phone calls were sworn by as effective methods to stay in touch with and engage donors. They are now being replaced by other information channels.

Don't get me wrong. Engaging in direct marketing and outreach is still important. However, when the conversation and communication channels change from one platform to another, you must go where the crowd is to stay relevant in this loud and competitive world. Otherwise, you might find yourself getting left behind.

How Other Nonprofits Are Using Crowdfunding

If you want to get a better idea of how the non-profit crowdfunding landscape is changing, take a look at these 10 statistics. They'll show you how non-profits are taking advantage of crowdfunding:

1. The average crowdfunding donation is $88.

2. On average, funds raised via individual charity fundraising pages earn less ($534.49) than projects run by a team that is crowdfunding for the same issue ($9,237.55).

3. Around 28% of donors are repeat donors.

4. December 3rd is #GivingTuesday! This online event was created to encourage people to donate to charity around the holidays. Online giving increased by 90% on that day from 2012 to 2013. The average online gift was $142.05.

If you have flexibility in terms of choosing the launch date of your crowdfunding campaign, just waiting to make sure that your campaign is live on #GivingTuesday, can help you do better. Doing a little research can help you figure out the best time to launch – and timing is important!

5. 42% of millennials give to causes that inspire them in the moment; they like to know how their donations will make a difference.

A lot of platforms allow you to create donation tiers which are a perfect way to explain to backers what different contribution levels will do for your charity or non-profit.

For example, An Hour of Code for Every Student (which raised over $5 million on Indiegogo in 2014), structured their reward levels to sound like this:

"At $10, you're bringing the Hour of Code to over 300 students! It only costs 3 cents/student impacted."

"At $30, you will bring the Hour of Code to 1000 students!"

You can see how this gives backers information on exactly how many students they will be helping with their donation. This encourages them to donate because they know that they will actually be making an impact in people's lives.

6. Fundraisers with a video raise up to 4x times more than those without videos.

7. In one survey, 55% of those who interacted with a non-profit on social media were inspired to take further action (donating money was the most common way that they did).

8. The top 3 online fundraising channels for non-profits are website donation pages (60%), social giving (19%) and portal donations (10%). You can check out the infographic below for more information.

9. In 2013, 30% of the $5 billion raised via crowdfunding went to social causes. Yes, the crowdfunding industry has gotten that big – and it keeps on growing!

10. Non-profits were 24% more likely to have increased their fundraising revenue from 2012 to 2013 if were accepting online donations.

How to Stay Up to Date With a Changing World.

In the next few chapters, I'm going to be covering a few of the newer fundraising techniques that have proven effective, including nonprofit crowdfunding and peer-to-peer fundraising.

I'm also going to be shining a light on online giving and how your nonprofit can grow it's following and maintain relationships with Twitter, Facebook, LinkedIn, and more. Finally, I'll discuss the importance of online video content and how to adapt your traditional marketing techniques to the changing online landscape.

The best thing about this new fundraising arena is that you don't need to be a technology savvy superstar to participate! As a cash-strapped nonprofit, the worst thing in the world is to hear that you need to be doing more with the few resources that you do have. Many of the tools and techniques that we are going to cover are free or extremely low cost.

Crowdfunding has become a great option for non-profits looking to supplement or move away from traditional fundraising methods. Charity and non-profit fundraising events are still very important (like walks, runs, bake sales, etc.), but establishing an online presence is crucial if your organization wants to stay relevant in a social media driven world.

Putting even a small percentage of your fundraising efforts into crowdfunding can make a big difference for your non-profit. In addition to actively engaging your audience on social media, you can learn how to increase your overall funding and raise awareness for your issue at the same time!

Chapter 2: Crowdfunding Success Stories

If there's one thing that I want you to get out of this chapter, it's that you can actually do this. You **can** raise money for your nonprofit with crowdfunding. You'd be surprised by the number of skeptical nonprofits that I speak with. There are SO many excuses as to why it's not possible or why it's too complicated. This is simply not true, and it's probably easier than you think.

Example #1: Sarah Kaufmann-Fink from MMORE

Multiple Myeloma Opportunities for Research and Education is a nonprofit organization that raised a staggering $88,015 to help #endmyeloma and expedite bringing a promising new study from the lab to the clinic.

I interviewed Sarah Kaufmann-Fink who is the inspiration behind the creation of MMORE and it's mission to support multiple myeloma research. In 2005 at the age of 22, she was diagnosed with multiple myeloma, which led her parents to start the nonprofit organization.

Although she responded well to her treatment and is currently in remission, Sarah is still a champion of the cause and was nice enough to give me an inside look into the fundraising campaign with [our podcast interview](#).

The organization decided to use CauseVox after carefully researching other peer-to-peer fundraising platforms. They wanted to keep costs low and hosting their own campaign on their own website would have added costs. It was their first full-fledged online fundraising campaign. They decided to do it during the month of March because March is Multiple Myeloma awareness month.

In total, the campaign received $88,015 from 14 personal fundraising pages that had 2153 donations. By fundraising pages, they mean the core group of donors that raised money on behalf of the organization. According to the website:

"CauseVox's peer-to-peer fundraising capabilities allowed individuals that were passionate supporters of the cause to create their own personal fundraising pages, share their stories, and distribute the campaign to their family and friends. This allowed MMORE to engage new donors organically and multiplied their former reach to include new networks, as well as build an online audience."

Example #2: Pencils of Promise and Invisible Children

Pencils of Promise is a nonprofit organization that builds schools and increases educational opportunities in third-world countries. Since 2009, they've built over 300 schools and helped over 30,000 students!

They launched a crowdfunding campaign using Classy for their Season of Promise. For just $25,000, you could build an entire school in Ghana, Guatemala, or Laos. The campaign ended up raising $1,271,141 of a $750,000 fundraising goal!

Another organization used Classy to launch an online crowdfunding campaign in 2012. Believe it or not, "Invisible Children leveraged the viral power of YouTube and the energy of Millennials to engage in a grassroots effort to locate and rehabilitate victims of the Lord's Resistance Army and to stop the war criminal Joseph Kony.

After the now-infamous KONY 2012 campaign video went viral, the organization raised $4.8 million on the Classy platform, solidifying it as one of the most successful nonprofit online campaigns ever."

Example #3: Food Share and the Salvation Army

Food Share is a nonprofit organization that's focused on feeding the hungry of Ventura County, California and educating the community about the root causes of hunger. They are also a member of Feeding America.

The organization used Mobile Cause to implement both online giving and crowdfunding solutions. They created a mobile-friendly donation button on their website (and text to donate abilities). They also set up a crowdfunding option for their corporate partners to raise funding from employees. Thus far, they've raised $425,000+ in one-time and recurring gifts and 1100+ donors have made online donations.

Another organization that's used MobileCause's fundraising functionality is the Salvation Army Boise. If you're not familiar, this org helps homeless, jobless, and poverty stricken families get back on their feet. Although the organization helps 70,000+ families annually, they wanted to do a Red Kettle Kickoff fundraising luncheon to boost donations.

"Board members competed to collect donations leading up to the event. Pre-event donations were displayed on the thermometer and after compelling storytelling, the speaker asked attendees to make mobile pledges."

After the event which had over 200 attendees, nearly $60,000 had been raised in the form of 163 donations. This was all in one hour!

Example #4: JFCS Annual Family Campaign and #DreamWithDAG

The great thing about crowdfunding is that it can also be used for annual giving pledges. The Jewish Family & Child Service organization helps "people overcome difficult life challenges so that they could go on to live fuller, more meaningful lives." In the past year, it touched over 1,000 lives!

They decided to adopt a new forward-thinking fundraising strategy and launch and online giving campaign for their annual family campaign using DepositAGift, another crowdfunding platform. They ended up raising over $76,000 from over 200 donors!

In addition, another campaign called "#DreamWithDAG: Cell Phones for Homeless Seniors" launched a fundraiser on DepositAGift in coordination with #GivingTuesday to provide cell phones to an often ignored poverty-stricken demographic. If you're not aware, #GivingTuesday comes the day after Cyber Monday and it collectively encourages businesses, individuals, and organizations to participate in online giving.

The campaign ended up raising over $10,000 and Lindsay Smith's organization, DOROT, was able to provide cell phones for homeless senior citizens as a part of their Homelessness Prevention and Aftercare program.

Example #5: Walk A Mile in Her Shoes and Police Unity Tour

I'm going to close out this list of examples of successful online giving campaigns with two successful peer-to-peer fundraising campaigns. First, let's talk about the Rape Crisis Center of Medina & Summit Counties. This organization is committed to ending sexual assault through education and empowerment. They launched a p2p fundraising campaign on First Giving for their 11th Annual Walk A Mile In Her Shoes-Akron (2016).

This campaign has raised $42,494 thus far, and is still raising money at the time of writing. There are 57 teams, 394 supporters, and 800+ donations have been made. Yes, the techniques, strategies, and platforms that I'm going to be mentioning in this book can be used *today* and are working *right now*.

The Police Unity Tour also raised money on First Giving for their 2016 tour. The organization is dedicated to spreading awareness about law enforcement officials that have died in the line of duty. They also support the National Law Enforcement Officer's Memorial Fund with monetary support.

With their 2016 campaign, they were able to raise $237,395 from 27 teams and 162 supporters. Overall, it ended up being over 2,000 donations! This campaign and the others mention in this list underscore the power of online giving, peer-to-peer fundraising, and crowdfunding.

So how can you use crowdfunding?

Let's be honest, many nonprofits are scrambling to maintain a sustainable business model. The age of grants are over and although it's true that corporate sponsors are willing and able to give, it's becoming even more challenging to stand out from the pack and develop lasting relationships that lead to dependable income streams.

Who would believe that you'd spend 75% of your time raising money every year and only 25% working for the segment of people you originally set out to help. As you've seen with these examples, you can use an online fundraising campaign to raise money for: annual giving, projects or causes, events, giving tuesday, and more. Let's talk about some more of the side benefits.

Generate Buzz, Media Coverage, and Great SEO.

Right now, crowdfunding is a hot topic. Nonprofits and causes that raise money through online platforms would not normally receive media attention, but since they are the forerunners in an emerging industry, they are shared, tweeted, blogged about to the point where everyone has heard of their organization and knows their story.

Try to see your nonprofit's crowdfunding campaign as both a way to raise funds and promote your brand. If you are successful in your campaign, you have a great story to tell and have a better chance of being covered by major media outlets. In addition, every supporter will tweet and share the fact that they pledged to your campaign. Not only does this spread awareness of your campaign, but it also lets people know about your cause and your organization's values.

Engage Your Supporters

Your supporters breathe life into your organization. Crowdfunding is a great way to establish a relationship with these men and women that share your values and goals.

Why not have your supporters play a larger role in your organization's future? With crowdfunding, you can give them the opportunity to engage your organization in a dialogue and provide their thoughts on your company's path going forward. Depending on your organization's focus, you may even be able to involve the supporters in the actual project so that they can see the results of their continued donations.

Grow Your Network

Growing your supporter base is a full time job. In a world where there are thousands of worthy causes, it can be difficult to make yourself stand out and really form those long-term supporter relationships that you can depend on. Crowdfunding can help you attract new supporters. Most nonprofit or cause-centered platforms cater to a niche audience of people who are willing to donate to causes that resonate with their values.

If someone is browsing a website looking to donate to a charity or non-profit, wouldn't you want to be listed on that website? Even if you do not secure a donation, it raises public awareness of your organization and lets people know that you are actively creating new projects to help communities around the globe.

Attract Corporate Attention

What better way is there to prove that your nonprofit's work has a major impact and resonates with the public than showing the numbers from your fundraising campaign to a potential corporate sponsor. Corporate sponsors are looking for engagement. Yes, they want results and the press, but it's also about the lives that your organization is affecting.

What are the demographics of your most-engaged supporters and those of the community you are helping? How can being a sponsor benefit the corporation, aside from making a positive difference in the world. When it comes down to persuasion, numbers are your friend and the more proof of engagement you have, the better.

Most nonprofits have supporters that are willing to donate a small amount each year. Think about how much you'll stand out if you have a group of loyal followers who tweet, share, and talk about how they donated to your crowdfunding campaign.

Gauge Public Interest

A meaningful social mission forms the foundation of an organization that creates change, but it's the way you go about making change that is key. Not all projects resonate with sponsors, supporters, and the community in the way that you'd like, even if the project resonates with your values. I hate to say it, but there is always a path of least resistance and sometimes you can affect the most change by selecting projects that have a strong base of support.

Creating a crowdfunding campaign is a great way to market-test project ideas to see the kind of traction that they can get with your donor base. This can be a key source of knowledge if you are considering pouring a large amount of money into a particular cause or are considering approaching a business sponsor for a particular project idea.

In the next section, I'm going to talk about some of the nonprofit crowdfunding platforms that you can use to accept donations online, take advantage of social media, and raise money for your cause or organization.

Chapter 3: Choosing a Platform

There are some awesome nonprofit crowdfunding platforms out there. I think it's inspiring to see some of the amazing projects that are being funded through online crowdfunding portals and the innovative ways that nonprofits are using crowdfunding to connect with their supporter base.

The internet is making it easier for donors to connect with meaningful social projects in their community and for local organizations to engage their supporters where they spend the most time! Facebook even has a "Donate Now" button for non-profit Facebook pages so that partners can collect money online easily from their user base.

Having been in a co-ed community service organization in college for several years (Alpha Phi Omega), I find this progress in fundraising technology really exciting! At the same time, with a flurry of new platforms and websites, it can be a headache for social entrepreneurs to identify how they can use these new engagement channels and which tools are good for their org's values and mission.

I think that one of the most common misconceptions about crowdfunding is that all platforms are created equal. They're not. There is a big difference between crowdfunding and peer-to-peer fundraising.

Crowdfunding vs. Peer-to-peer Fundraising.

As a non-profit organization, you would typically use crowdfunding to fund projects or new initiatives. The target audience for the fundraising campaign would be both your usual donor base and individuals around the web. For this type of campaign, you would need to actively market the fundraising campaign to your established supporter base and to potential new online supporters.

Typically, most crowdfunding campaigns consist of: a video pitch, a written pitch, and reward tiers. Reward tiers are perks or items that your donors or backers will have access to, should they pledge a certain amount of money. For example, if you are running a fundraiser for a new school in El Salvador, if they pledge $20, they may get a hand-written thank you from one of the students, along with the student's photograph.

Benefits:

- You can access a larger audience than your usual donor base.
- You can attract media attention for your new endeavor, which will benefit your organization.
- You can offer "rewards" or "perks" that engage your supporters in the new project.
- You can more easily track fundraising patterns through the platform's analytics.

Drawbacks:

- You need to coordinate shipping rewards for individuals that donate at various fundraising tiers.
- You need to spend time creating a marketing and PR strategy for the campaign and execute on it.
- You need to create a video and come up with reward ideas.
- You may risk public failure if your campaign doesn't go well.

Peer-to-peer fundraising is a bit different than traditional crowdfunding. As an organization, you would not use peer-to-peer fundraising to collect donations for a project or new initiative. Instead, you would use a peer-to-peer fundraising platform to empower your employees or supporter base to raise money for a specific cause on ***your*** behalf.

For example, if you were organizing a marathon, some of your participants may want to raise money for your charity through friends and family that would like to sponsor their effort. You could partner with a peer-to-peer fundraising platform to offer them an easy way to collect these donations. The platform would give them a fundraising page that they could then market to their social network.

Benefits:

- Easy to use out of the box solution for empowering participants or supporters in your community to raise money from their friends and family.
- There is no marketing required to individuals on your part as an organization. It is up to the individuals using the peer-to-peer fundraising platform to market their own campaign to their local network.
- The individuals using the peer-to-peer fundraising platform do need not to overcome a credibility barrier, because their friends and family know them and their character.

Drawbacks:

- If your supporters are using peer-to-peer fundraising to raise money for your organization, you don't directly have an effect on the outcome of funds raised. It's your job to teach your supporters how to fundraise for you.
- You will only reach new donors through your existing donors
- You will need to do a lot of hand-holding with your supporter base.

Keep in mind that there is a bit of overlap between crowdfunding and peer-to-peer fundraising. For example, the way that Ethan Whittington raised money for a Boston homeless man initially seems like it would be more of a peer-to-peer fundraising endeavor via GoFundMe, but it was picked up by the press and donations poured in across the internet. He ended up raising over $150,000.

Usually, for cause-related crowdfunding campaigns like the one mentioned in the previous paragraph or "fund my life" kind of projects, the biggest barrier to receiving donations is that you need to convince backers why it is a worthy cause and why they should care. If you are able to, then like I mentioned before, you can access a larger audience than your usual donor base.

But, the focus of this ebook is on crowdfunding for nonprofits, not personal crowdfunding campaigns. If you're interested in raising money for personal causes like medical bills, travel expenses, or even your wedding, you can check out my other Amazon ebook here.

Finally, the last option is for you to host and run a crowdfunding campaign on your own website! This will give you more control over the design of the initiative, how visitors interact with it (like including an email opt-in), and it will let you capture all of their traffic information via google analytics. It will also cost less, as most platforms take a percentage of funds raised.

Of course, it takes a little bit of technical savvy to pull this off and you will need to actively market the project, but the payoff is huge. Rather than interacting with a 3d party website, visitors will be coming to your website.

Which type of fundraising is best?

This really depends on a few things. First, if you are planning to make use of a peer-to-peer fundraising platform, then you need to ask if you have an established base of donors that would be willing to take the time to raise money from their friends and family for one of your initiatives. In my opinion, they would be more willing to if they were a part of the initiative, like a relay or a marathon, where the donations go to charity.

I find that the traditional form of crowdfunding tends to work better when there is a defined project with objectives that will have a measurable impact. Remember, you must set a fundraising goal. It's not as good for raising $X amount on a recurring basis every month for a particular charity. In that case, you may want to think of creating a specific fundraising page on your website, rather than having a project that is part of a larger external platform.

Lastly, as enticing as it may seem to set up a crowdfunding page on your own website, it's a lot of work. You must have a strong understanding of the technology that goes into accepting online donations. You don't want your website to go down during the middle of the campaign due to an influx of traffic or faulty programming. I wouldn't recommend this route, unless you really know what you're doing.

Nonprofit Crowdfunding Platforms

1. Razoo. Razoo lets users launch a crowdfunding campaign for any cause that they care about. They were founded in 2006 and since then have helped individuals and nonprofits raise more than $500 million for various causes.

2. Causes: This website is for people who want to change the world. Categories vary from disaster relief efforts to human rights. Causes has raised more than 30 million for non-profits. You can use the website to discover, support and organize campaigns, fundraisers, and petitions around issues that impact you and your community.

3. Buzzbnk: A UK platform that supports social entrepreneurs and innovators. "Positive People Backing Bright Ideas."

4. StartSomeGood: StartSomeGood empowers "social innovators," and forwards the trend of social entrepreneurship.

5. Kickstarter: A project crowdfunding website that any organization or individual can use to finance their event or project. You can launch a Kickstarter campaign as a nonprofit, but you can't say that you'll be donating the funds that you raise to a specific charity. Every campaign on Kickstarter must be for a project, not a cause.

6. Indiegogo: An international crowdfunding site for creative types that can also be used to raise money for charity and non-profit organizations. Indiegogo also has Generosity, which is used for personal crowdfunding campaigns.

7. Pozible.com: An Australia-based website that encourages creative projects and ideas. This website can also be used for charity purposes.

8. MobileCause: While not a traditional crowdfunding platform, MobileCause gives nonprofits the software tools that they need to raise money in the form of a crowdfunding campaign. You can use it to set up text-to-give campaigns, fundraise for events, or launch a nonprofit crowdfunding campaign.

Peer-to-peer Fundraising Platforms

1. Classy

Classy was founded in 2011 and is a crowdfunding and peer-to-peer fundraising platform that can be used to create a donation page for specific projects or year-round initiatives. The software also allows you to sell tickets and track registrations for events. *"Empower your community by adding personal and team fundraising pages."*

2. CrowdRise

CrowdRise was founded in 2010 and is another tool that you can use to create a p2p fundraising campaign and enlist your supporters to raise money from their crowd. Like Classy, you can also manage charity events with integrated registration functionality.

"Crowdrise is meant to complement your Charity's website. Online fundraising is the fastest growing segment of personal giving and Crowdrise can help you tap into this rapidly growing market in unique, value-added ways."

3. FirstGiving

FirstGiving is an older fundraising platform that was founded in 2003. You can use their software to help your supporters become advocates for your charity project or cause and reach out to their own social network. The platform also offers the capability for donors to cover the website's processing fees.

"FirstGiving enables nonprofit and fundraisers alike to meet and exceed their goals of raising money for important causes, building awareness, and expanding the world of giving."

4. CauseVox

CauseVox, founded in 2010, is an online crowdfunding and fundraising platforms for nonprofits. You can use it to create a simple fundraising page without needing to customize the code or deal with APIs. CauseVox also features personal and team pages, where *'supporters can easily create their own personal page on your CauseVox site and raise donations on your behalf.'*

5. Razoo

Razoo was founded in 2006 and is a crowdfunding platform for cause. It was announced in 2013 that they now offer peer-to-peer fundraising functionality. You can create a team page where you can invite donors or supporters to help raise money for your cause.

"A team page on Razoo unites multiple people who are fundraising for the same cause or event. Complete with a leaderboard, one-click fundraiser templates, and a real-time donation and comments stream. Teams are ideal for any race or charity event, like marathons, bike rides, and service trips."

Which platform should you go with?

This is a tough question to answer. First, you're going to have to assess the type of functionality that you're going to need for the campaign. The functionality of a nonprofit crowdfunding campaign is very different than a text-to-give campaign, which is very different from a peer-to-peer fundraising effort.

Next, you'll need to look through the websites that have this functionality and explore how their platform and processing fees differ. You'll also probably like the design of some websites more than others. Not every platform is created equal.

As you can see, there are a lot of options to choose from and there is no one blanket "best" platform. It all comes down to your needs as a nonprofit organization. Personally, I think that when it comes to raising money online, the platform matters far less than the marketing strategy.

Your marketing strategy is going to have a bigger impact on whether or not you successfully raise funds than the platform that you choose to launch on. This is exactly why I've dedicated the next few sections of this ebook to creating, marketing, and getting the word out about your campaign. I'll walk you through how to stand out from the crowd. I'll show you the best practices for turning visitors into donors. Finally, I'll include a video at the end of this ebook that will continue to educate you about raising money online for your nonprofit organization.

Chapter 4: Making a Great Campaign

I'm not going to lie. The makeup of your crowdfunding campaign has a huge impact on whether or not you're able to successfully raise money online. Even organizations who have a devout following and strong brand recognition still need to put together a well-constructed campaign page. But, there's so much more.

There's this huge misconception out there that your website is there to "describe what your nonprofit does," or that your campaign page is there to "show people what you're raising money for." Newsflash! Your website is there to **sell**. Your campaign is there to **sell**. I'm not talking about selling products. I'm talking about selling visitors on your mission, your goals, the merits of your cause, and your ability to change the world. The name of the game is ***persuasion***.

As we go through each element that goes into a successful crowdfunding campaign, I want you to keep this word in the back of your mind. When you're putting together your campaign page, think to yourself, "How will this video or that image help turn website visitors into donors? What emotions will it evoke?"

Rule #1: View your campaign page as a sales page

A "sales page" or "landing page" is marketing jargon for a page that influences a visitor to take a pre-determined action. That action could be to buy your product, subscribe for future updates, or attend an event. This is labeled as a "conversion."

I know that this sounds basic, but actually it's really important. The biggest factors that are going to affect your conversions, and therefore nonprofit crowdfunding success, are:

1. The type of traffic you drive to the campaign page
2. The layout or makeup of that campaign page.

Every piece of content on that campaign page, whether it's text, video, or photos should be designed to influence the visitor to take action.

While yes, your page will be informative, it should also be focused on selling your organization to donors and potential partners (even if you don't admit that).

I'm going to put together a brief checklist of items that you're going to need to get together. I'll be exploring specific items more in-depth later.

Main campaign checklist:

1. A compelling pitch video with an attractive thumbnail (2:30 - 5 minutes)
2. Images for the page to demonstrate points, share your story, and evoke emotions
3. Rough schedule of updates you'll be sharing throughout campaign
4. Possible rewards or "perks" for donors to choose from
5. Copywriting-optimized text to share your story and other information

Supporting action items:

1. Educational materials for core supporters to explain your campaign, for peer-to-peer fundraising especially.
2. Set up social media accounts and make rough schedule of social media messages, images, and videos. I use Buffer to schedule my messages and the Pablo tool to make quotes for my Instagram.
3. Content for social media and relationship building (short videos, blog posts, etc). Canva is a great tool to create easy well-designed images.

4. Media list of reporters/journalists in your niche. I'd use the Chrome App Boomerang to schedule follow-ups.
5. Accompanying website/domain name. You could use Wordpress, SquareSpace, or others to set up your website.
6. Set up email marketing account to store subscribers. I use MailChimp to collect emails and LeadPages to create landing pages.

Every piece of content is going to not just introduce donors to your organization, but also to you and your brand. Presenting your pitch is a unique opportunity to give visitors a chance to "get a feel for you" and what you're all about. I'll talk a lot more about marketing in chapters 5 and 6.

Rule #2: You're going to have to do a lot of handholding.

This is true of both nonprofit crowdfunding campaigns and peer-to-peer fundraising campaigns. Education materials are a must, no matter what kind of fundraising effort you run for your nonprofit!

Let's be honest, not everyone is tech savvy, and even those who are may have never given to an online fundraising website and don't know that they should share the campaign when it's out.

It's important to be thorough when preparing guides to: pledge/donate, share on social media, get involved, etc. Although you will have the opportunity to include some information on your crowdfunding page, I would supplement this with material on your website.

Education materials don't just need to take the form of "how to contribute" to your campaign, but they also explain more about your cause or initiative. They can highlight why people have decided to give to the project and the compelling reasons why people are involved with the nonprofit.

Although it may seem obvious to you why such and such a cause is important, it may not to others until you explain to them why with compelling stories, videos, or articles which they can discover in their Facebook feed, email inbox, or other social media channels.

Make it as easy as possible for your core supporters and even your employees to just "copy and paste" your marketing and share it with their network. Of course, you should underscore that they can also customize your message by sharing why **they** love your cause or organization. However, many donors simply don't have the time or knowledge to come up with something great to say. In these instances, having a core base of educational materials that they can draw from really helps.

This honestly goes as nitty gritty as having suggested messages for them to share via email or Facebook and flyers that they can just print out and share in their hometown.

The MMORE charity did a killer job of this in their campaign, which I covered on my blog and podcast. Multiple Myeloma Opportunities for Research and Education is a nonprofit organization that has raised a staggering $86,000+ to help #endmyeloma and expedite bringing a promising new study from the lab to the clinic.

MMORE provided a wealth of information for donors to draw on including: press releases, social media post templates, FAQs, fundraising letters, and more (no pun intended). I'll break down the skeleton of their education materials.

Fundraising Support (for P2P fundraiser)
- Some tips to help make fundraising as simple as possible
    - Downloadable press release to send to journalists in your local area
    - Downloadable Facebook cover photos
    - Mini-fundraising event planning advice
    - Downloadable fundraising letters

- Tips on how to set up your fundraising page
    - Step-by-step instructions with screenshots
- Accepting cash or check donations
    - How to accept donations in different circumstances
- Common donor questions and answers
- Promotional photos/materials
    - I'd recommend materials for FB, Instagram, offline/online marketing.
- Information about the research/cause.

All of this material was provided on a page on their website to help fundraisers as they're going about raising funds for MMORE.

Rule #3: Study the best practices.

There are best practices when it comes to putting together an effective crowdfunding video. Ultimately, your video should be on the shorter side, but the real question that you need to answer is whether or not potential donors ever tune out during the length of your video.

Naturally, most people who are interested in a cause have little more than a 3 minute attention span before they begin to lose interest or their mind begins to wander. However, as you must know from browsing around the web, some videos are more engaging than others. There are a few ways that you can maintain interest and engagement over the course of a video pitch, which I'll discuss below.

Ever notice how television shows and movies are constantly changing the scene, camera angle, or flashing to another take? By changing the angle or direction of the camera view every 10-20 seconds at minimum, you'll make the viewing experience more interesting and keep the potential donors attentive.

Also, using humor throughout the video to make the viewer chuckle will not only improve the chance that they'll share the video with a friend and say something like "This is hilarious you must check it out," but it will also increase the amount of time that they watch the video, because there is a promised future emotional reward. This is why humorous YouTube compilation videos can be long and also popular. Obviously,

Music, good lighting, and a passionate speaker are also great ways to set the emotional tone for the video and make the backer want to learn more about the cause.

What Points Should You Cover?

The video is meant as a teaser, a pitch, or a trailer that will introduce you, the product, and why it matters. Backers can always look through your campaign text for more information, but there are some key points that every crowdfunding video should cover.

Tell a story. Stories are an integral part of the human experience and a good story will even captivate strangers.

Why did the team or you create this organization? This will help backers get to know you, your values, and get them excited about your cause.

How are your donors a part of this journey? Why are you bringing this project to the world and what will your donors enable you to do?

Bring credibility to your project by shining a spotlight. I hate to say it, but your video is one of many. How do you stand out? One way you can stand out is to use your video to show your viewers the impact that your organization/initiative is having. This could mean featuring multiple people in your video or highlighting testimonial reviews.

Finally, each video should have a clear call to action. This means, give your donors a reason to give to your project. Don't just ask for money! Ask them to join you on a quest. Invite them to become a part of your community. Challenge them to change the world with you.

How should backers feel after watching your video?

Before answering this question, I'd like to bring attention to the emotions that a human being must feel to share a product or piece of content with their social network.

An infographic created by CoSchedule highlighted that there are 5 core reasons why people share content online. This data was drawn from The New York Times Customer Insight Group.

Entertainment: 49% say sharing allows them to inform others of things they care about and potentially change opinions or encourage action.

Define ourselves: 68% share to give people a better sense of who they are and what they care about.

Relationships: 78% share information online because it lets them stay connected to people they may not otherwise stay in touch with.

Self-Fulfillment: 69% share information because it allows them to feel more involved in the world.

Support a cause: 84% share because it is a way to support a cause or issues they care about.

In addition, there are specific types of emotions that are commonly associated with viral content.

- Curiosity
- Amazement
- Interest
- Astonishment
- Uncertainty

Keep in mind that you might not be able to appeal to all of these emotions in your crowdfunding video. However, I would pinpoint what you want potential backers to feel after they watch your video.

For example, they might feel angry about a cause you highlighted and want to help, inspired about how your organization can change a friend's life, entertained and have the desire to be entertained more by supporting your nonprofit, or feel a sense of awe or amazement and say to their friends "this is so cool!"

So what's the format?

Aside from the information that I've highlighted above, I would split your video in the following way.

- 10% humorous or entertaining.
- 40% on the pitch and story
- 30% showing your personality (passion, values, approachability, etc).
- 10% bringing credibility to the project.
- 10% the direct sales pitch or ask to donate to help support the cause.

The video is going to be one of the most important parts of your campaign. However, these are also some best practices when it comes to the copywriting or actual "text" of your crowdfunding campaign.

Use headlines appropriately

There's a reason that textbooks, newspaper articles, blogs, and magazines use headlines to separate blocks of text. It makes it much easier to scan through the content and pick out sections that are relevant to you. It seems like a no-brainer, but many campaigns I see read like long essays. Make it easy for people to go through the elements of the pitch with descriptive and eye-catching titles so that they don't look at long blocks of text and close the browser window.

Short and point-driven paragraphs win out

Ideally, the first sentence of every paragraph should encompass the primary point you are trying to make. Each sentence following the first sentence should support or elaborate on this point. When you are finished with this point and would like to introduce a new topic (or expand on your topic with supporting points), a new paragraph should be created.

For example, this sentence and new paragraph would be a supporter to my previous paragraph and by making it a new block of text, it's easier on the eyes and makes the pitch much more scannable.

Bolding, Links, and Italics are your friend

You might not think it, but when people are scanning an article or pitch, their eyes really do gravitate towards bolded words, links, and italics. Use these tools to convey tone or emotion with your pitch.

Break paragraphs up with images

As stated previously, long blocks of text aren't just bad organization, but they really turn people off from whatever it is you are trying to communicate. Simply put, they are confusing and intimidating. Don't give your readers a reason right off the bat to close their browser window! Break up your paragraphs with relevant images and illustrations.

Emotion & passion trumps "professionalism"

Many people who come from a strong schooling background have this erroneous idea that it's wrong to use "I" when writing for a reader or that terse, sterile sentences convey professionalism, and are therefore best.

While it's true that for some audiences, extreme formal writing is required, the goal when running a nonprofit fundraiser should be to foster empathy and connection with potential donors.

People love intense passion and in a big-business social media driven world, individuals want to connect with other individuals more than ever. The companies and people who win out are the ones that that can establish rapport or genuine one-to-many relationships with their customer base.

Show your backers how passionate you are. Share your vision.

Put the backer first

If you are using the words "me," "I," "mine," etc...You should only be doing it 10-20% of the time. During the rest of the time, the focus should be on YOU. How does the campaign benefit your donors or the people you're helping. How will their life be awesome because of this campaign. Why will their contribution make this project a reality and ultimately change the world for the better?

Read your pitch out loud

Writing is just another form of communication and your goal in composing a crowdfunding campaign should be to communicate your vision and idea to another human being (while getting them excited about it in the process). There's no worse way to keep yourself at a distance than to use stilted language or incorrect grammar.

Read your entire pitch out loud. Are you using language and grammar that you would use if you were speaking to someone in person?

Rule #4: Involve your donors in the campaign

There are a lot of ways to involve your donors in your upcoming crowdfunding campaign. On the simple side, you can share updates with them, celebrate milestones, and show them all of the cool things that you're doing leading up to the launch of the campaign. In fact, updates should be a major part of your overall campaign to maintain momentum and to continue to generate interest.

Another way to involve your donors is to create perks or rewards that they can claim after they donate to your campaign. Not every crowdfunding platform supports rewards, but many do! Some will even let you choose from pre-determined rewards, like a discount at a well-known coffee shop, that you can then offer your donors.

Just remember that as you're going about creating these rewards that you're going to have to factor in the costs of making good on these promises. If you're going to be sending out physical thank-you cards, there are costs associated with that!

In conclusion, there certainly fundamental core principles of a great crowdfunding campaign. If there's one rule that I could boil it down to, it would be to pay attention to what emotion your campaign evokes, because this will determine whether or not people choose to take action. Still, we haven't actually yet covered the most important part of the crowdfunding campaign. Marketing! That's what I've devoted the next two chapters to, along with many tools and resources that you can use to simplify the process.

Chapter 5: Mastering Donor Psychology

I've been thinking about my online business career, and I think that you can sum up my overarching mission in one sentence. My goal is to get people to take ***action***.

There's a term in the marketing world called "vanity metrics." These are metrics that simply don't matter in the long run, but that will boost your ego in the short run. This could include things like the number of visitors to your website, the number of times your message has been shared on social media, or glowing emails from people who say that they love the mission of your nonprofit.

While these things might make you feel good, they are complete bull****. At the end of the day, the only thing that matters is whether or not you've gotten donations for your fundraising campaign. Have people actually taken out their credit card and donated money?

In this chapter, I'm going to be reveals several key psychological techniques that can be used to get visitors to take action. These are the same strategies that master marketers use to sell billions of dollars-worth of product a year to consumers around the world.

Rule #1: Social Proof Creates Trust and Lowers Defensive Barriers

I'm a pretty normal young man living in NYC. I don't smell, I'm reasonably intelligent, and I'm told I have a nice smile.

But, if I were to go up to a random person on the street and say "Hi, nice day, right?" more often than not, I'd get looks of confusion, suspicion, annoyance, and many people would nervously smile and rush past.

I know this because I actually do this sometimes just to work on my social skills and face social fear.

People are naturally suspicious in our culture of strangers and organizations that we haven't heard of before. It's because the person **suspects** that the other person wants something from them, which puts them on the defensive and raises their guard.

There is no familiarity, trust, or value in the interaction. Also, everyone else is on their way to work or another destination, so it feels "weird" for them to respond to or stop and talk to a complete stranger. It's an interruption.

Social proof is one way to jump this barrier and gain instant trust. Here's how Wikipedia defines it:

"Social proof, also known as informational social influence, is a psychological phenomenon where people assume the actions of others in an attempt to reflect correct behavior for a given situation. This effect is prominent in ambiguous social situations where people are unable to determine the appropriate mode of behavior, and is driven by the assumption that surrounding people possess more knowledge about the situation."

When a product or individual has social proof, others will approach them from a perspective of **curiosity** rather than skepticism.

They're more likely to take a second to watch your video or read your fundraising page because "other people think it's interesting, so I might as well check it out."

It's basically thinking that just because a book is bestselling that it's probably good and worth buying. You might even take less time to check it out than a non-bestselling book.

If you've ever seen a bunch of people surrounding one person in a group setting, I'm willing to bet you thought, "Is that a celebrity?" or you were more apt to go and join the crowd yourself to see who they were.

When you lead with social proof, rather than being skeptical, the prospective donor is more likely to focus on the mission, story, or awesome impact that your organization has had. They'll be curious instead of suspicious.

There are a few ways to create social proof, including:

- Testimonials
- Genuine activity and donations
- Comments section
- Media hits/write-ups
- Social sharing
- Reviews/emails
- Credentials and endorsements

While increasing the vanity metrics that we discussed earlier shouldn't be your main goal, they can be leveraged to grow your social proof or credibility in the minds of new or existing donors.

Increasing the social proof of your organization or your crowdfunding campaign is one way to get visitors to take action. A campaign with high social proof is more likely to convert browsers into donors. Rather than clicking off your page, a donor is going to open their wallet and put in their credit card information.

The worst thing that could happen is that a visitor comes to your campaign and sees 0 donations, 0 social shares, and a half-baked "ask." It makes them feel like little real work went into putting together the fundraising page. They'll rationalize that either the organization isn't serious, that the cause isn't worthy of their funds, or that something else is wrong, because no one else has given money.

On the flip side, if someone discovers your campaign online and sees a bunch of donations pouring in or massive engagement and social sharing activity, they're more likely to take a sec to watch your video and read through your pitch. The fact that other people are paying attention to the fundraising effort makes them want to learn more. It evokes curiosity and engenders a stronger feeling of trust. We're going to revisit this topic when we talk about marketing your nonprofit's online fundraising campaign.

Rule #2: A Sense of Urgency is What Prompts Action

The reason that people **take action** is because there's an impending deadline or other event, which creates a sense of urgency.

I don't know about you, but I was definitely one of those kids who procrastinated most of the college semester and then crammed two days before the exam. Many of my nights were spent in the library the day before a final paper was due.

Of course, the best and most *rational* thing to do is to plan, take action according to your plan, and see the desired result. But, most people aren't rational. We're guided by our emotions.

When someone feels a sense of urgency about a particular activity, they will:

- Focus and drone out distractions.
- Take massive action in a small amount of time.
- Overcome hurdles that would normally set them back.
- Pay less attention to hindering emotions or thoughts.
- Look to short-cut signals to make micro decisions.
- Take more risks.

I've written and spoken extensively about how a nonprofit's fundraising meter will grow and flatten out over time. Many campaigners see an influx of donations towards the beginning and end of their campaign. Both of these events create a sense of urgency among supporters, whether it's to claim limited quantity "rewards" or get in before the doors close on your campaign.

The best nonprofits are able to prompt action throughout the duration of their fundraising campaign. But, the great thing about crowdfunding is that the basic model ***encourages*** urgency due to the temporal nature of the fundraiser.

It's your job, as a campaign manager, to communicate this emotion to your backers, so that they feel this urgency. Don't just assume they'll feel it. Communicate it. Repeatedly.

The more you create a sense of urgency in the minds of your donors and campaign visitors, the better the chance that they'll actually take action and give money to your case. Of course, this is assuming that you put together a great campaign page. Even with a great page, you'll still raise money, but when you effectively communicate urgency, you'll raise even more money.

Rule #3: Build Relationships at Scale

Okay, I get A LOT of emails and many of them start like this...

"Hey Sal. Love the blog and podcast. Tell me, how do I get strangers to back my campaign?"

First of all, I don't do consulting at the moment and always direct people to my FREE online content. I only provide advice if it benefits the community, like on my forums or the comments section. I wish I could provide it one-on-one, but I simply don't have enough hours in the day.

Second of all, you can't get strangers to back your campaign. However, you can turn strangers into FRIENDS and then get them to back your campaign. It's a subtle distinction.

The way you do this is by building relationships at scale.

Here's the idea summed up. Since everyone thinks ***you*** want something from them, break the pattern by giving them something

they want. It has to be something they actually want and it has to add value to their life in some way.

As you begin to provide quality content, advice, or free value, the people will begin to feel like they know you. When someone watches a free video that you put together, they'll get a sense of your values, and eventually, they'll develop an emotional connection with you.

This is EXACTLY why we feel like we "know" big-name YouTubers or celebrities and are completely okay shouting out their name in public or buying something they endorse. In fact, I'd go so far as saying that we feel like we "love" certain comedians because we relate with them so much and almost consider them to be a friend.

We're willing to watch a 5 minute video created by a random person in the world if it makes us say "wow," laugh until we cry, or if it resonates with us and inspires us to be a better person.

When you put out content in the form of videos, emails, social media posts, blog posts, or images that educate, inspire, or entertain, you're investing in the relationship with your potential backers and customers.

Ultimately, you're doing all of this simply build relationships with multiple people at once. A thousand people can watch one video on your Facebook page and come away feeling like they know a bit more about you and your organization. This is powerful. In the past, you'd have to directly interact one-on-one with the same number of people to create that type of response.

When you do this over a span of time, you can get 1,000 people to subscribe to your email list, or to follow you on a particular social media channel. I know it works, because I've used it to build my own email list to over 20,000 subscribers. I've used these techniques to grow an online forum to over 6,000 users, get over 100 positive iTunes reviews for my podcast, and make a living doing what I love. By the way, I'm a millennial. When I started, I didn't have what older people label as "experience." If a kid can figure this out, so can you. I'm also giving away the formula. You just have to copy it. Remember, all of this is what gives you the leverage that you need to CRUSH IT during the first week of your nonprofit's crowdfunding campaign.

Rule #4: Stories Trump Logic

When is the last time that you sat through a two hour long YouTube video lecture? Probably never (though if you have, that's awesome!).

But, people around the world are 100% okay with sitting through a 2 hour movie in a dark room. Even if the movie sucks, they'll stick around because they want to find out what happens.

The same goes for TV shows. How many times have we heard friends say "okay, let's just see what happens and then we'll change the channel." We'll default to this even if it's a trashy show or it isn't good, and we pretty much know what's going to happen.

Stories are powerful for three reasons:

- They create anticipation
- They hold attention
- They encourage empathy with the characters and challenges

If you want someone to feel *exactly* how you felt in a given situation, weave a story around that event. Don't just tell them how you felt.

Quite simply, the best stories **communicate information** and make you **like** or at least feel close to the main character. They are a powerful vehicle for creating trust online.

Not only are they a great way to get people excited about taking action and joining your campaign's community, but they are also super good for seducing journalists and bloggers like me to write about you!

Many of the successful crowdfunding campaigners that I've had on my podcast pitched me with a compelling story, which I then wanted to share with the podcast listeners.

I hate to break it to you, but no one is going to remember the statistics you put out, not even your key donors. Statistics are an important way to establish credibility, but they aren't great for arousing strong emotions. But, I can almost guarantee you that EVERYONE will remember a compelling story. The more emotions that someone feels, the more likely they are to remember an event and also take action in the moment.

You should be sharing your story though several mediums and across multiple platforms. I'm not just talking about the social media platforms out there. I'm also referring to your email list, and when you're speaking at events.

A great story will bring listeners into your world, and when they feel what you feel, they're more likely to take the action that you think "makes complete sense." For most nonprofits out there, that's to fight for a particular cause or to right some injustice in the world.

Rule #5: Create the Emotion of "Liking"

Okay, I know that I sound like I'm a robot right now. I really do enjoy analyzing emotions with the rational side of my brain. I also must ***strongly emphasize*** that the techniques I'm sharing in this post should only be used if you genuinely believe that you have an amazing product that will make other people's lives better.

In Robert Cialdini's seminal book, Influence, he reveals 3 key points, that I'll highlight below:

- "We like people who are similar to us in terms of opinions, personality traits, background, or lifestyle."

- "Familiarity also plays a role in decisions. Seeing or experiencing something more and becoming familiar with it leads to greater liking."
- "A halo effect occurs when one positive characteristic of a person dominates the way that person is viewed by others. We assign favorable traits to good looking people without logic."

In case you missed kindergarten, when we like someone we are more likely to help them, support them, and take the time to listen to what they have to say.

I'm not saying that you should try to force people to like you or to not be genuine. I'm saying that you should be aware of the emotions that your words, imagery, video, and content creates.

Making a joke in your video might make **you** nervous, but it might make **them** laugh, feel good about themselves, and like you more.

If you're speaking to a group of programmers, you're probably going to generate a great feeling of "liking" if you yourself are also a programmer, can make inside jokes, or relate to the job lifestyle. If you're a business guy who doesn't know the first thing about programming and you assume certain things or butcher key terms, it's unlikely that the audience will see you in a favorable light.

Being focused on how much your donors like you or your team is another great way to avoid typical objections that bog down many nonprofits.

For example, a skeptical donor might harp on the negative qualities of online giving with regards to credit card security. Let's be honest though, online security is a reality. This is innovation we're talking about. You then have to deal with that objection.

If that donor likes you, then they are going to approach the campaign from an entirely different mindset. Maybe instead of focusing on ***that*** particular aspect, they'll smile at what you're trying to accomplish, decide to support it, and rationalize that you're a good guy so you will be forthright with issues that you or they encounter.

Of course, you should be 100% transparent and forthright with any complications. Just keep in mind that the degree to which someone likes you will affect how they rationalize the things that you ask of them.

To sum it all up, you don't come off as some faceless organization with a big board of directors that is just looking to raise money. Personalize it. You want to come off as an actual human being, and in the best case scenario, as a likeable friend.

These key rules form the bedrock of a sound marketing strategy, which I'll be covering next. You should always have them at the back of your mind when you're engaged in donor communications. They're used every day by marketers to sell products to the public. They aren't just for businesses though. You can steal them and apply these techniques to getting visitors to take action and donate to your online fundraising campaign. They're proven to influence the only thing that matters, getting your donors to ***take action***.

Chapter 6: Marketing Your Campaign

Online marketing is one of the most confusing subjects out there. Not only are there a slew of different social media platforms, but the demand for a donor's attention is stretched thinner than ever before. You have to compete with funny cat videos on Facebook, entertaining YouTubers, Instagram fitness models, and more for the only thing that matters, a prospective donor's **attention**.

Thankfully, I've figured out the best ways to market a crowdfunding campaign and I'm going to share them with you in this chapter. These are tried and true techniques that are proven to work! Keep in mind that every campaign is different. You might find that you're seeing more results through one marketing channel than another. Don't worry! This is a **good** thing. Half of the battle is figuring out where your audience is and how to reach them. The other half is figuring out what they care about.

The three main ways to get attention online. I like to segment the online audience into a few different categories. Ultimately, these buckets come down to how people spend their time on their laptop and on their smartphone. A good marketing strategy will incorporate all of these elements, but the first is the most important.

Rule #1: Your Email List is King.

Your email list is the Holy Grail of all of your marketing activity. Why? According to Mckinsey & Company, "Email conversion rates are three times higher than social media, with a 17% higher value in the conversion."

The individuals who sign up for your email list are not simply numbers, part of a statistic on your email provider's dashboard, or passive donors. They are real human beings with thoughts, feelings, desires, and emotions.

Email is still the #1 marketing channel out there for getting donors to take action. It's completely replaced the old-school way of sending out marketing messages to physical mailing addresses. Think of email as the "home-base" where most donors receive information about the topics that they care about.

Tomorrow, Facebook could change their algorithm so that no one sees your posts. Your website could be hacked. You could find that your Instagram profile is banned for some reason. But, you'll always have your email list.

If you have 1,000 people subscribed to your email list, then 1,000 individuals have raised their hand saying, "I want to receive messages from your nonprofit organization." Think of a room with 1,000 people in it. That would be a massive crowd!

The reason that email is so powerful is because it allows you to direct traffic to a **designated place** at a **specific** time. You don't have to wait for people to see your messages on social media, which might be drowned out by all their other social media messages. Instead, they can all check out your crowdfunding campaign at the same time and make a donation. This is why many campaigns see so much activity and so many donations during the first day of their launch, which usually spills into the next two days.

In order to get more email subscribers, you need to understand a bit of the psychology behind subscribing to an email list.

Use an email list provider, not a temporary solution.

I know that money is tight, which is why you're planning on launching a crowdfunding campaign in the first place in order to finance your nonprofit organization! However, it would be a huge mistake to not use an established email list management provider, like MailChimp, which is free up until 2,000 subscribers, or

Aweber, which has been around for a while and has great functionality.

Why? Email list software will:

- Give you analytics every time you send a campaign regarding the number of people who click links, open that email, unsubscribe, and more.
- Let you create auto-responders every time someone opts into your email list to direct them to a page or convey a message (like the one I've set up with my newsletter).
- Make it super easy to set up a series of pre-scheduled messages, which can be a great way to automate some of the marketing process as you lead up to the launch of your campaign.
- See who most frequently opens your emails.

Offer value in exchange for an email address

What is "value?" You're right. That's a very abstract concept.

Basically, by giving your potential subscriber something exclusive or beneficial, he or she will be more likely to subscribe to your email list because they will get something out of the relationship.

For example, you could use MailChimp to direct the subscriber to:

- A behind-the-scenes special video.
- Deliver an exclusive invite to a fundraising gala.
- Send them a link to a poll or special FB group where they can vote on something related to your organization.
- Get an exclusive discount code that will give them 10% off of the products or services of partner companies.
- View an awesome hilarious company video "beware: don't watch this video for our upcoming fundraising campaign while you are at work, or you will burst out laughing."

Think of these value-adding ideas as mini rewards that are meant to gain the interest of a potential subscriber so that they are more comfortable exchanging their email address for future announcements regarding the launch of your nonprofit's fundraising campaign.

Make your email-opt in noticeable.

Ask yourself three questions:

- Where is the email opt-in form on your website?
- What is the first thing that should draw a visitor's attention when they visit your site?
- Why did a visitor come to your website in the first place?

Now, ask these questions to a series of visitors that you've connected with (friends, family, individuals who are interested in your project).

You might know where your email opt-in form is, but do they? You might want to direct their attention to a particular video, link, or email opt-in form the moment that they visit your website, but what actually is grabbing their attention?

Determining how your visitor discovered your website in the first place, whether it was through social media, a search engine, an article you've written, or an event you attended, will help you figure out the type of content that you should offer them in exchange for subscribing to your newsletter.

For example, if someone discovered your website from an inspirational video that you posted on social media, which will be a part of a larger online awareness mission, then it's likely that they'd love to receive more content like this!

Resources to help track this information:

- Google analytics.
- Bitly links.

- CrazyEgg heat map and click tracking.
- Mouseflow mouse tracking.

Use call to actions (ask people to subscribe).

This might seem silly, but you'd be surprised the amount of email subscribers that websites lose out on simply because they forget to ask a visitor to subscribe!

One way to put this in perspective is to watch YouTubers who have millions of subscribers and who have made a living out of making online videos. What's the last thing that they say at the end of every video? It's something along the lines of "if you enjoyed this video, take a moment to give it a thumbs up or leave a comment." They might also say "subscribe if you'd like more funny prank videos like this!"

ABSYL: Always be selling your list, meaning, always be highlighting why people should subscribe, particularly if they've taken the time to watch one of your videos, read through a blog post, or go visit your website.

Don't just tell people what you want, which is to subscribe to your email list. Explain to them why it's awesome for them if they subscribe.

Build a landing page

A landing page is very different from a full-blown website, which has all of the information about your team, your mission, and your journey. The purpose of a landing page is to solely to collect an email address or have your visitor take an action, rather than exposing them to lots of information about your company or project.

You might set the landing page as your homepage leading up to the launch of your nonprofit's crowdfunding campaign or even have a custom domain name that you reference on business cards or should you attend any conventions, do interviews, or get linked to by a media publication.

A great landing page will share compelling information about your upcoming project in an organized fashion and highlight any multimedia that you have (video, images), the benefits of being a participant in your upcoming your launch or what's meaningful about the mission, and more.

Tools to help you build a landing page:

- LaunchRock
- Unbounce
- LeadPages
- OptimizePress (if using WordPress – more complex).
- Free: Use WordPress and a landing page theme.

Consider WordPress-Based Plugins

If you're not using WordPress as the framework for your website, then this step won't be helpful. However, if you are, then I highly recommend checking out the OptinMonster and OptinSkin plugins, which I use on this website and others.

If you're using MailChimp as your mailing list provider, you could also enable "evil popup mode," but I don't find this to be as affective in terms of providing data or cool themes as the above two plugins.

These plugins will draw more attention to your message which prompt visitors to subscribe to your email list.

Drive traffic and measure results

I've highlighted a few tools and techniques to get more email list subscribers in anticipation of your crowdfunding campaign launch. Ultimately, the only way to get more subscribers is to drive traffic to your website or landing page and adjust the positioning/wording of the call-to-action messaging that you're using to get a visitor to subscribe to your email list.

This could mean that you might need to use trial and error to figure out the type of incentive that gets a visitor most excited about signing up for your email list, or the content that you're putting out to get people on to your website in the first place.

Rule #2: Have a social media presence everywhere, get followers, and automate.

The nonprofit industry is historically slow to adopt new technologies. Instead, organizations stay with tried and true methods, like mailing out brochures to potential donors in a community. Investing some time to learn how to build up followers on your social media accounts will be well worth it in the future when you have a bunch of interested individuals with whom you can share your new campaign!

I'd define the main social media networks as:

- **Facebook.** Facebook is one of the largest social media networks out there with 1.71 billion monthly active users in 2016. Key trends are mobile adoption, video consumption on Facebook, and the changing Facebook algorithm.
- **LinkedIn.** LinkedIn is the largest professional social network with 450 million members. The platform has growth a lot in the last few years, with the introduction of articles and content on the website.
- **Instagram.** While I don't think Instagram is as mature as Facebook with paid marketing tools, it's still a very powerful network to gain followers and get people interested in your cause.
- **Twitter.** Finally, many have argued that Twitter is a waning social network, but I don't agree. There are still a large number of people who get their news from Twitter and check it daily.

You could also look into networks like SnapChat and Pinterest, but I wouldn't include these in the main list. Ultimately, you'll probably narrow in on one or two of these social networks in the long-run. My Twitter is certainly much stronger than my Instagram. You'll find the network that is the best fit for your organization, but you should have a presence on all of them!

Now that we've outlined most of the major networks, you're probably wondering...how are you actually going to get followers? How are you going to get people to take time out of their day to follow you and receive messages related to your nonprofit organization?

You won't be using social media to share thoughts like "My cat just rolled over." You will be using social media as a tool to figure out what type of content your audience likes and what causes they care about.

As a rudimentary example, let's say you are trying to start a nonprofit to help educate children in El Salvador and you shared a post on Facebook of a child and his mother reading, which also had an inspirational caption. If it got lots of clicks and shares, that tells you that potential donors are moved by images like these.

You may consider creating similar content on your nonprofit's blog and then sharing it. In the long-term, it would attract readers to the blog, who are also part of your donor base. You will then have the opportunity to ask them to donate to your upcoming crowdfunding campaign.

There are two words that sums up why people will follow you: content marketing.

You're going to be putting out content that will either be informative/useful or entertaining. Informative content could take the form of articles, tips, ideas, and advice that you share to help them achieve their goals in some way. Entertaining content could take the form of quotes, images, shocking or inspiring facts, etc.

This type of content is emotional. People will follow you based on how they perceive you will make them feel in the future. You may make them feel inspired, motivated, or hungry to reach their goals.

By continually putting out free content that resonates, you'll begin to build an audience on these different social media platforms. Yes, this takes time. Accumulating followers and improving audience engagement doesn't happen overnight. If you're just getting started, plan for this to be an eight month to a year-long process before you begin getting some momentum. In that span of time, you will figure out what types of content works best for your audience, when the best time to post is, which social media channels are a good fit for your nonprofit, and you will gain an in-depth understanding of the problems that your customers care about.

Eventually, you'll start to mix in your own "call to action" messages on social media, like asking people to back your crowdfunding campaign. But, you shouldn't start here. The primary focus should be to get people to follow your social media profile to get notified when more content comes out.

I've used this simple strategy to build up thousands of followers on Instagram, Facebook, and Twitter. However, it does get difficult to keep up with all that work! That's why I've automated most of my social media marketing.

Tools to automate your social media

I'm horrible at being consistent. Even my tennis coach used to say, "Sal, you need to be more consistent! You're great one day and have a bad day the next."

Thankfully, when it comes to social media marketing, there are lots of tools out there that will allow you to pre-schedule social media messages that will go out in the future. This means that you can sit down and spend two hours planning out all the social media messages that will be shared on your Facebook page for the next month. Then, you don't have to worry about it for the rest of the month.

I'd recommend looking into:

Hootsuite: A powerful social tools to save time managing multiple social networks. If you haven't heard of it, it's a tool that you can use to schedule Tweets and Facebook posts ahead of time on your phone or on your computer.

Buffer: Buffer is a Hootsuite competitor and lets you manage your Twitter, Facebook, and LinkedIn social profiles. Buffer makes it super easy to share any page you're reading. Keep your Buffer topped up and it will automagically share them for you through the day

The great thing about these two tools is that they also come with analytical capabilities. I personally use Buffer, which tells me how many people are clicking on the links in my posts, sharing them, and which posts are seeing the most engagement. I can also re-schedule posts to go out.

Rule #3: Get free traffic from the media

Leveraging a media is a great way to get free traffic to your nonprofit crowdfunding campaign. First, I'm going to cover what to include in a press release. Second, I'll talk about direct outreach. Last, I'll cover a few press release tools out there.

When drafting a PR campaign for your crowdfunding campaign, it's important to keep in mind how crowdfunding differs from the launch of a traditional fundraising event. Although there are a lot of crowdfunding sites out there, many of them have the following elements in common.

Fundraising Duration: Almost every crowdfunding campaign has a set duration, which will impact the amount of time that you have to take advantage of any PR attention or media hits. Therefore, you need to be super organized when drafting a PR outreach strategy. Some media publications will offer the "embargo" option if they like your project and want to write about it. Basically, this means that they will hold off on the publication of the article until a certain date.

Rewards and Perks: The rewards and perks offered throughout a crowdfunding campaign are a great way to incentivize lurkers to become donors. Some of your donors might care about the mission of your project, like you, or find your video engaging. Others will simply want to learn about what kinds of perks you're offering. Make sure to include these in your press release. Also, underscoring the "limited" or "scarce" nature of them and how to claim one is a great call to action for people to check out your campaign.

Social Proof: Backers are more skeptical than ever! Unfortunately a growing number of campaigns have defrauded donors or have simply not fulfilled on their promises. Therefore, any way that you can add social proof or credibility to the campaign will make it more likely that journalists will check out the project or that potential backers will. Social proof can include the number of social shares, donors, comments, or dollars given. Credibility can include media mentions, partner organizations, or simply a compelling founder story.

Here are a few items that you should keep in mind when creating the PR draft for the launch of your crowdfunding campaign.

Do you have an eye-catching headline? In the same way that click-bait news headlines give readers a reason to click through the story, you want to have an interesting headline for your press release and the subject of your email so that a journalist has a reason to read further.

Have you included images or multimedia? Words are one way to tell a story. Images and video are other ways to get a story across very quickly in this social media driven and attention starved world. Have high resolution images on hand that the journalist or blogger can use in their article. Often times, the number of images or multimedia you can send is limited, so provide a link where they can find more multimedia assets.

Are there quotes from the founder or team? Have you ever noticed how news or human interest stories tend to include quotes from sources or the founder themselves if it's a new nonprofit organization? Rather than making the journalist call you up or exchange emails for an interesting quote, include that quote in your press release! You can also include testimonials from donors or partners to add to the social proof of the pitch.

Is it easy to find relevant links and contact information? I can't tell you the number of times that I've been emailed asking to cover a story and the email didn't have a link to the company's website or the URL of where I can find the campaign. Make it as easy as possible for journalists to find where your campaign exists online. They might be on their mobile phone and not want to search around to find it.

Have you answered the who, what, when, where, why and how? It's true that the press release should spin an enthralling story and make the journalist envision how awesome of a story this would make. However, it also needs to include concrete facts, like when the campaign will end (or start), what the product is, who designed it, and why they are so passionate about this project.

How hard to read is the press release? It's always best to put yourself in the shoes of someone reading the press release. Is the information easily digestible? Are the paragraphs short and to the point? Are you using active verbs and strong grammar? One easy way to get an idea of how well it's written is to read it out loud! You'll quickly catch any grammar or spelling errors. You'll also get an idea of how the sentences flow.

What emotions do you arouse in the reader? Finally, a press release is part art and part science. Ask a friend in your industry (or familiar your industry) to read your press release and ask them how they feel after having read the story behind the fundraising effort. Are they excited to learn more? Bored? Are they confused? Simple questions like these will give you an idea of the tweaks you might need to make to elicit the desired emotional response.

With your press release, you need to identify how your latest crowdfunding campaign fits into the hot topics and trends that journalists and bloggers are writing about.

For example, right now, teaching coding in inner-city schools is gaining traction. There are niche blogs writing about programming, education, and STEM. There are also larger publications creating content about the technology industry.

If you created a nonprofit crowdfunding campaign to help educate kids about coding, you may want to consider contacting publications that have written about these topics, as you are a prime example of a growing trend and therefore newsworthy.

Again, how does your story fit into the overall global discussion? What trends are you a part of? Research the publications engaged in these trends.

The other thing that I'll say before we get into contacting journalists is that you must appeal to multiple audiences.

Does your nonprofit organization use a new teaching technique that will have a big impact on a particular industry? What organizations will benefit down the road if your campaign raises the needed funds?

For example, when Arnold Schwarzenegger was working to attract media attention for his breakout film Conan the Barbarian, he appealed to multiple audiences in order to get the ink needed to fill theaters.

"To promote the movie, it was important to work every possible angle. We used special-interest magazines to build an audience – stories on sword fighting for the martial-arts magazines. Stories for horse magazines. Stories for swords and sorcery. Stories for bodybuilding magazines on how you needed top conditioning to be Conan." – Total Recall: My Unbelievably True Life Story

Let's start to talk about how you can directly contact journalists and get them to write about your crowdfunding campaign. Email is still the preferred method of contact, but I've also seen campaigners get media stories by contacting journalists via Twitter and LinkedIn.

How do you stand out from the crowd?

According to a survey conducted by BuzzSumo, Journalists receive 25-100 pitches via email per day and countless more on social media. In order to stand out, it's best to avoid cliché buzzwords and stick to a succinct, straight-forward, and relevant pitch

Be succinct. Get to the point, and if needed, use bullet-points to highlight the major reasons why this news is important and a good fit for the publication. Don't write an essay. Your email should be scannable.

Be straight-forward. Avoid PR buzzwords that only serve to make it more difficult to understand your story and why it's a good fit for the publication. Otherwise, you will sound like all the other nonprofits pitching the journalist and fail to stand out.

Be relevant – Why this journalist, why your company, and why does this story matter now? Don't just copy and paste generic emails. Tailor your pitch to both the reporter and the publication.

When is the best time to pitch a reporter?

After conducting several informal interviews, PrDaily put together an awesome breakdown of the best time(s) to reach out to a journalist. Overwhelmingly, all of the reporters surveyed preferred to be pitched via email in the early morning. However, due to the large volume of weekend mail, the participants also suggested to wait until Tuesday, once the Monday rush was over and they had more time to look over each email.

This information is corroborated by MarketConsensus, who also recommended sending pitch emails between 8 am – 11 am and to avoid Mondays.

Should you send mass emails and if so, when?

Despite the overwhelming industry advice not to send mass emails, I've actually responses from them and have gotten stories as a result of them. Many journalists may not like these practices, but they can work if you have a killer headline, pitch, and are going after a bunch of publications with a similar audience.

However, I do think they should be used in conjunction with direct pitching and relationship building. That being said, if you're going to send out a mass email with services like PRWeb, MyPrGenie, PRNewswire, SBWire, or others, then take into account the best time to send that email. **S**ubscribers' top engagement times are 8 a.m. – 10 a.m. and 3 p.m. – 4 p.m. with up to 6.8% average open rates and CTR (click through rate).

PR goes to experts in their space

Sometimes when you're marketing a new fundraising effort, it's easy to forget that you're in "this" for the long haul, whether that's growing your nonprofit or starting a new one.

In my experience, experts in their space will never have to worry about getting PR. What was the first thing that happened on TV when Malaysia Airlines Flight 370 disappeared? The media brought aviation experts on to comment about the event and the implications.

Experts are cited in the media all the time! Even I was quoted in a recent CNN interview. The important thing is to put yourself out there as an expert, so that you can seize these opportunities for some free PR.

HARO is a great free resource for these types of PR hits.

How can you frame yourself as an expert in your space and use that as an angle for a story, or to get some free PR indirectly?

87% of Reporters love data, facts, and figures.

Have you ever noticed when a "new study" is released that analyzes data points to corroborate or highlight an interesting trend, it goes viral on news outlets?

How can you enhance your pitch with facts, figures, and data? How does your nonprofit fit into a larger cultural trend?

Backing up your vision and story with numbers is a great way to snag attention away from other pitchers, just pushing their "game changing" initiative.

P.S. Just kidding about the 87%

Journalists must write about things they don't want to.

I'll tell you a little secret. Journalists don't necessarily want to write about every story, but sometimes they have to.

You're really going to tell me that if a holiday is coming around, like Christmas, that a publication isn't going to look for Christmas stories? Or if a particular story is blowing up like the Potato Salad Kickstarter, an editor isn't going to say "I want this story on my desk by ____."

Newspapers are in the business of attracting eyeballs and advertisement dollars. Most major publications always need to write about what is trending, or be left out of the flow of online and mobile traffic.

The question is: How can you fit yourself into the stories that are trending or a holiday that is coming up? You need to begin to think about what kinds of stories reporters will be looking for given the time of the year and what's happening in the current media discussion.

Repeat business = success.

There is a big difference between a nonprofit organization that has repeat donors and one-time donors. The same is true for PR. Rather than seeking one-time transactional relationships, it's best to develop a long-term relationship with a journalist, who may move publications in the future or be able to forward you along to his or her friends (who are also journalists).

You should take a long-term view of PR outreach. Why? This is exactly what a PR agency does, and they are in the business of getting their clients stories. Why wouldn't you take the same approach as a professional PR firm?

A relationship with even a handful of reporters can yield dividends down the road. Going out of your way to be helpful and connecting them with sources or people in your industry they'd like to speak to can be a good way to start.

Your headline must be clickable

It's hard to have a clickable headline without knowing your audience, which brings us back to point #1 (relevancy). Ideally, your headline should be tailored to the individual reporter or publication.

Your name and headline are the first few things a reporter is going to see when they look at your email. How can you phrase the headline to get them interested in learning more?

One technique I've found to be helpful is to see if there are any headline commonalities in other articles that have been published by that reporter and then craft your email subject to be similar to those headlines.

There is no blueprint.

Although there are "best practices" and mistakes to avoid, getting PR is a learning process. You need to figure out what works well for your company and your industry, which will take time.

Personally, I've had experiences that fly in the face of the common industry advice in terms of the ideal times to send emails and how to best do journalist outreach. Keep in mind that these are general guidelines, and are not set in stone.

I think the most worthwhile takeaway you should get from this article is that you need to adopt a PR mindset.

You need to begin to observe the news, TV, and print media and begin to form questions. Why did a publication quote this expert, or why did this reporter choose to write about this particular story? Beginning to make yourself aware of the inner-workings of the news media will help you begin to become active on the pitching side

Press release websites:
- CrowdfundingPr.org (free)
- PRLog (free)
- Free Press Release (free)
- 188PressRelease (free)
- 24-7 Press Release (free)
- Pr.com (free)
- i-NewsWire (paid)
- PrWeb (paid)
- PrNewswire (paid)
- BusinessWire (paid)

In this chapter, you discovered a few surefire ways to market your upcoming crowdfunding campaign, along with a few key tools that you can use to make the process much easier. These techniques will only work if you take action and actually implement them! You have to start now. Start building your email list, social media profiles, and start developing a relationship with journalists. You'll thank me later!

Chapter 7: Starting a New Nonprofit

Starting a nonprofit organization isn't too different from starting a new business. There are best practices, mistakes to avoid, and ways to improve the chance that you're one of the few nonprofits that survives and prospers, rather than one of the many that fail.

Before we get into the legal and financial realities of running a nonprofit organization, I want to break down the fundamentals of why nonprofits exist and how to ensure that yours prospers amidst so much competition.

Every nonprofit solves a problem that people care about.

It's easy to get lost in the romantic notion that your organization *must* exist to right some wrong or help a group of people that sorely need assistance. I want you to take a second and turn off the emotion-centric side of your brain and turn on the rational side.

Every nonprofit exists for two reasons. First, it solves a problem or services a need among a particular target audience. Your overall success will be determined by the degree to which you generate results with your efforts and improve the lives of this community or group of people. It's very important that you nail down how you'll identify these metrics so that you can show your donors that you're having a genuine impact.

For example, let's say you want to help educate people in third-world countries. That's a very broad goal. While that might be your end mission, how can you narrow that goal in the short term? For starters, let's pick one country, say, El Salvador. Now, which demographic are you looking to educate? Youth? Single mothers? Rural families? What subjects will you teach to them and by what means. Are they going to learn how to write better English from a Spanish textbook, or learn better farming practices from an on-site mentor?

Specificity is power. The more specific that you can be about your target market, the easier it will be to come up with metrics that you can track. These are statistics and numbers that you'll be able to show to potential donors to convince them that their hard-earned money **can** make an impact in the lives of these individuals.

The second reason that a nonprofit exists is because it solves a problem that people care about. Wait...what? Did I actually just say that? Yes, I did. Not everyone cares about every problem in the world. The degree to which people care about solving a problem will influence the amount of funding that you can get, the quality of people who will work for you, and the overall success of your nonprofit, as defined by the improvement of your key metrics.

There are many reasons that potential donors might care about a problem. Likely, it has affected their life in some way or they empathize with the particular group of people for a key reason. I'd recommend going back to the chapter on donor psychology and exploring it in-depth. But, caring extends beyond donors. Not everyone who cares about your problem is going to give money to your cause. However, they may engage in other activities like helping you push legislation forward, share messages on social media, and help rally more members to your cause.

If no one cares about the problem that you're trying to remedy with your nonprofit, then it's going to be a big uphill climb. You're going to have to convince the world that they should care. To be quite honest, I'd recommend exploring other ways to tackle the problem rather than trying to launch a full-scale awareness campaign, which would take a lot of money and time. I would focus on a smaller subset of the problem or on a cause that your donors **do** care about that relates to the cause you **actually** want to tackle. This will help you build some street cred so your organization is strong enough to take on the major problem when you're ready. You'll then have enough resources to spread awareness about it.

Nonprofit startup checklist

Let's drill down some of the components that you're going to need to master when you're starting a new nonprofit organization. I hope that this will serve as a go-to checklist that you can reference at a later date. I'll also be mentioning some of the resources that you can use to make the entire setup process easier.

1. Website: Many of the nonprofits that I've worked with have struggled on the technical front. I want to make it easy for you to set up your website, gather email addresses, and have a strong online presence. No matter what anyone says, people *will* judge you by the design or appearance of your website. It will affect how much they trust you and how seriously they take you. Here are a few different options for setting up your website.

Wordpress + Bluehost Hosting - Wordpress is one of the easiest ways to set up a new website because of the myriad of free professional-looking themes and various plugins to expand the functionality of your site. Most people think of blogs when they hear about Wordpress, but it runs many company websites, ecommerce sites, and more.

SquareSpace - SquareSpace is probably the best alternative to Wordpress if you don't want to host your own website. I like SquareSpace because of the beautifuly designed templates that you can choose from. They also have good analytics and an intuitive user interface. The only downside about SquareSpace is that if at some point in the future you want to host your own website, you'd have to migrate all that data off their servers.

Wix - Wix is an alternative to SquareSpace with great templates and functionality that you can implement to set up an attractive website for your organization. It's pretty easy-to-use and straight forward. Again, this is a good solution if you're new to the web and don't want to host your own website, but it's not so great if you want to host your own content in the long run.

You can use any of the above three to set up your professional website. The only other thing I'll say is that it's crucial that you obtain your own domain name. Once you set up your website, you must collect email addresses from your visitors. This will help you communicate with your core audience and direct traffic to your campaign once you launch. Here are a few tools to help you set up an email list.

MailChimp: MailChimp is a email service that lets you collect email addresses, create email lists, send out campaigns, and track their results. You can see who opened your emails and how many people clicked your links. It's an amazing tool for reaching out to your audience via email, which is still the highest converting source of donations online. At the time of writing, it's free up until 2,000 subscribers.

Aweber: Aweber is a great alternative to MailChimp that also allows you to build, track, and communicate with an email list. I can't underscore how important it is that you start to collect an email list of your donors. You'll thank me later. It's an extremely powerful way to get everyone to take action at a specific date and time. At the time of writing, you can start a 30 day free trial.

2. Social Media: Did I just hear a collective groan? Haha! Soo many of my readers and podcast listeners have told me that they don't even know where to begin with social media. Before you try to skip past this section, let me say one thing to you.

It's 100% okay if you don't use social media for your personal life, but you're 100% a fool if you don't use it for your nonprofit. There. I said it!

Social media is free traffic to your website and awareness for your organization. It's one of the best tools out there to connect with donors and share your message with the world. But, even I will admit that it can be time consuming. That's why I'm going to share two different tools that you can use to automate the entire process. These will make it so much easier to manage your various social media profiles and track their results. Just so we're clear, I'm talking about accounts on Facebook, Twitter, Instagram, YouTube, and LinkedIn. Depending on the mission of your organization, you might explore others like SnapChat, Pinterest, and Reddit.

Buffer: Buffer allows you to manage your Twitter, Facebook, LinkedIn, and other social profiles. You can use the service to schedule posts to go out in the future so that you don't have to worry about sharing social media posts next week. These posts can go out at a specific time every day or at a time that you designate. You can also track the activity on your posts, including traffic, reach, and engagement. There is a free plan at the time of writing.

Hootsuite: Hootsuite is another tool that lets you schedule social media and helps take the burden off consistently pushing out awesome and engaging content. At the time of writing, on the free plan, you can connect up to 3 social media profiles and get basic analytics and reporting for how your social media posts are doing (clicks, shares, etc).

3. Funding: We've already talked a lot about getting funding for your nonprofit in this book using crowdfunding and peer-to-peer lending. But, I also wanted to highlight some of the other avenues out there like writing grants, soliciting big donors, and hosting offline fundraising events.

Nonprofit Fundraising 101 by Darian Rodriguez Heyman is a good introduction to raising money for your nonprofit and has a received a lot of praise from Amazon readers.

Fundraising For Dummies by John Mutz and Katherine Murray is another Amazon book that gives you a basic overview of the nonprofit fundraising world. While online giving is certainly the future, it's still important to examine traditional fundraising techniques and ways to build relationships with donors.

4. Legal Classification: Many nonprofits will organize as a corporate entity to give liability protection to the officers and directors. After filing the Articles of Incorporation, nonprofits then obtain 501(c)(3) status, meaning that they are exempt from federal taxes. Some states will also allow these organizations to be exempt from sales, corporate, and property tax. In exchange for receiving these benefits, there are restrictions placed on the activities of the nonprofit. You'll also have ongoing compliance duties. You must apply to the IRS for recognition by filing Form 1023 (or Form 1023-EZ). Lastly, 40 states and the District of Columbia require nonprofits to register with the Department of Charities before soliciting any donations from the public.

I highly recommend [checking out this webpage](#) which breaks down the state-by-state filing requirements for incorporating a nonprofit.

5. Financial realities: The Nonprofit Finance Fund's annual survey asks nonprofits in the US about their financial health. Of the 4,749 respondents in 2015, 24% ended 2014 with an operating deficit and only 29% broke even. In fact, of the 1,091 respondents who had a budget deficit, 18% of respondents experienced a deficit of greater than 10%.

I want to give you a clear picture of the financial structure of the majority of nonprofits out there. Unfortunately, of 4,439 respondents, 53% have 3 months or less of cash on hand. Can you imagine the stress that you'd feel in this situation? As you might guess, according to the in-depth survey, the great challenge of most nonprofits out there is long-term financial stability.

There is one other bit of parting wisdom that I'd like to leave you with to splash some cold water in your face before you go about putting in all the hard work to start a nonprofit. Even if you are lucky enough to secure government funding, you won't always receive government payments on time. Only 52% of respondents to the survey by NFF stated that federal payments were received on schedule. 41% reported that state payments were received on time. 45% indicated that local payments were received on time. In all of these cases, the main way that nonprofits managed this deficit was by using reserves or a line of credit.

Clearly, the financial realities are tough. Changing the world is tough. The good news is that between 40-50% of nonprofits have consistently reported that they could not meet demand for services and programs in their area. This means that there is a lot of opportunity to help out in-need demographics.

Before you take the leap and start your nonprofit, take a second to read through the 2015 State of the Nonprofit Sector survey. You'll thank me that you did.

6. Organizational Structure: Arguably, this is the most boring part of setting up a nonprofit, but it's also the most important. Your leadership team can make the difference between success and failure. When you invite members to become a part of your board, you'll instantly have access to their social networks, which is a powerful asset!

Your board of directors is responsible for the vision and mission of your nonprofit. They are separate from your management team, which carries out the day-to-day operations of the nonprofit. Ultimately, they'll help keep your organization on track and accountable to its goals.

There are many ideas about how the board should operate, but in general, you'll need to assign roles for the Treasurer, Secretary, and President. Any individual can become a board member, however, it's important that they realize they have a legal duty of care and duty of loyalty towards the organization. They could be sued for not adhering to these responsibilities.

Rather than seeing the organizational structure, rules, and guidelines as a "hurdle you must go through" to set up a nonprofit, I'd see them as an asset. At the end of the process of recruiting and signing on board members, you'll have a team of diverse backgrounds, interests, and who each have a different network that they can use to get more donors for your organization. Strong relationships with your board members will pay dividends in the future. As long as you make sure that each member is passionate, committed, and value-producing, the board will serve as a competitive advantage to your nonprofit that will improve its chances of long-term survival.

Should you start a nonprofit?

Only you can answer this question. You're now aware of just how difficult it is to launch a new nonprofit organization. It's going to be like climbing a steep mountain. But, the good thing is that you're not alone. You can always shoot me an email or hit me up on Twitter to ask questions or discuss topics! If you're truly passionate, willing to work hard, and completely determined, then I think that starting a nonprofit is an amazing challenge and will give you life changing insights!

Chapter 8: Conclusion

Online giving is going to continue to grow. If you master it now, you'll reap the benefits for many years to come. Still, you can't just read about it. You actually have to get out there and take action. This is all a learning process. Later, you'll thank me that you took the first step towards developing new donation streams for your nonprofit.

As much as I enjoyed writing this ebook, I can't wait to bring you more content about nonprofit crowdfunding and peer-to-peer fundraising! Whether you're setting up a new nonprofit, or you've been running one for a while now, I want to continue to help you on your journey.

Below, I'm going to link to a FREE webinar that I've put together to introduce you to nonprofit fundraising.

FREE: [Nonprofit Crowdfunding And Online Fundraising Webinar (https://www.youtube.com/watch?v=9wIZkJ5a62E)](https://www.youtube.com/watch?v=9wIZkJ5a62E)

This is a webinar that I conducted with another fundraising professional. I hope you find it to be helpful!

Good luck on your journey!

- Sal

P.S. If you enjoyed this ebook, please take a second to leave me a positive review on Amazon! Thanks!

About the Author

Salvador Briggman founded the popular blog, CrowdCrux, which has been cited by the New York Times, The Wallstreet Journal, CNN, and more. He helps entrepreneurs raise money on crowdfunding platforms like Kickstarter and Indiegogo. Last year, he helped nearly 400,000 individuals raise money from the crowd through his website, products, newsletter, and forum.

Made in the USA
Middletown, DE
20 July 2017